Thoughts in the Presence of Fear

was originally published on OrionOnline, Autumn 2001.
http://www.oriononline.org

The Idea of a Local Economy

was originally published in *Orion* magazine, Winter 2001.

In Distrust of Movements

appeared in *Orion* magazine, Summer 1999. It is adapted from
a keynote address delivered at the 1998 Northeast Organic
Farmer's Association conference

In the Presence of Fear
by Wendell Berry

ISBN 0-913098-60-4

The Orion Society
187 Main Street, Great Barrington, MA 01230
telephone: 413/528-4422   facsimile: 413/528-0676
email: orion@orionsociety.org   website: www.oriononline.org

Cover image: Photograph of Mark Spencer's painting, *Blue Baroque (Hope)*, by Joe D'Alessandro. Photo courtesy of the Gerald Peters Gallery, Santa Fe, New Mexico, and Mark Spencer.

Designed by Jason Houston

Funding for this publication has been provided by a generous grant from the Geraldine R. Dodge Foundation

Printed on New Leaf Reincarnation Matte paper.
100% recycled, 50% post-consumer, process chlorine free.
Printed in the U.S.A. by Excelsior Printing Co.

2nd printing

In the Presence of Fear

Three Essays for a Changed World

by Wendell Berry

a publication of The Orion Society

In the Presence of Fear

Foreword

In the aftermath of September 11, 2001, The Orion Society asked Wendell Berry and several other regularly contributing writers to *Orion* and *Orion Afield* magazines to send short essays that offered their reflections on the unfolding crisis, which we then published on OrionOnline.org. The response to the series was immediate and nothing short of extraordinary. Clearly the collection of essays, which we called *Thoughts on America: Writers Respond to Crisis*, had struck a chord.

It would not be an overstatement to say that one of the pieces, Wendell Berry's "Thoughts in the Presence of Fear," has become an instant classic. In the first month alone, OrionOnline received reprint requests from dozens of publications that reach audiences in over seventy-five countries, and the piece was translated into seven foreign languages. Yet for those familiar with Mr. Berry's work, the forceful sensibility and precise language of this poignant essay is a timely distillation of values that he has expressed throughout his career. For this reason, and recognizing the monumental urgency of the times, not to mention the evident public thirst for authentic wisdom in the face of tragedy, we offer this collection of three related essays by Wendell Berry.

Each of these essays appeared in Orion publications: "Thoughts in the Presence of Fear" on OrionOnline, and "The Idea of a Local Economy" and "In Distrust of Movements" in *Orion* magazine. Whereas "Thoughts in the Presence of Fear" is especially notable for its brevity and timeliness, "The Idea of a Local Economy" expands upon the notion of a vital local economy as a crucial counterweight to the ill effects of an emerging Techno-global Age. The third essay in this collection, "In Distrust of Movements," eloquently dismantles long-held assumptions about movements that, in their singularity of purpose, do not promote a comprehensive vision for broad-based cultural change.

As Mr. Berry states in the first lines of "Thoughts in the Presence of Fear," "The time will soon come when we will not be able to remember the horrors of September 11 without remembering also the unquestioning technological and economic optimism that ended on that day." September 11 will undoubtedly come to represent an attack on those things that are worst about America just as it was an attack on what is best. And as July 4, 1776 and December 7, 1941 have become essential touchstones for the American identity, so will September 11, 2001 become a date by which we measure our progress as a nation. Our hope is that, in the months and years to come, our nation will live up to the dreams and expectations of our founding fathers, and that we will duly reinvent ourselves in the image of a more just, less materialistic, ecologically secure and spiritually enriched culture.

Marion Gilliam   Laurie Lane-Zucker
Chairman   Executive Director

Thoughts in the Presence of Fear

I.   The time will soon come when we will not be able to remember the horrors of September 11 without remembering also the unquestioning technological and economic optimism that ended on that day.

II.   This optimism rested on the proposition that we were living in a "new world order" and a "new economy" that would "grow" on and on, bringing a prosperity of which every new increment would be "unprecedented."

III.   The dominant politicians, corporate officers, and investors who believed this proposition did not acknowledge that the prosperity was limited to a tiny percentage of the world's people, and to an ever smaller number of people even in the United States; that it was founded upon the oppressive labor of poor people all over the world; and that its ecological costs increasingly threatened all life, including the lives of the supposedly prosperous.

IV. The "developed" nations had given to the "free market" the status of a god, and were sacrificing to it their farmers, farmlands, and rural communities, their forests, wetlands, and prairies, their ecosystems and watersheds. They had accepted universal pollution and global warming as normal costs of doing business.

V. There was, as a consequence, a growing worldwide effort on behalf of economic decentralization, economic justice, and ecological responsibility. We must recognize that the events of September 11 make this effort more necessary than ever. We citizens of the industrial countries must continue the labor of self-criticism and self-correction. We must recognize our mistakes.

VI. The paramount doctrine of the economic and technological euphoria of recent decades has been that everything depends on innovation. It was understood as desirable, and even necessary, that we should go on and on from one technological innovation to the next, which would cause the economy to "grow" and make everything better and better. This of course implied at every point a hatred of the past, of all things inherited and free. All things superceded in our progress of innovations, whatever their value might have been, were discounted as of no value at all.

VII. We did not anticipate anything like what has now happened. We did not foresee that all our sequence of innovations might be at once over-ridden by a greater one: the invention of a new kind of war that would turn our previous innovations against us, discovering and exploiting the debits and the dangers that we had ignored. We never considered the possibility that we might be trapped in the webwork of communication and transport that was supposed to make us free.

VIII. Nor did we foresee that the weaponry and the war science that we marketed and taught to the world would become available, not just to recognized national governments, which possess so uncannily the power to legitimate large-scale violence, but also to "rogue nations," dissident or fanatical groups and individuals—whose violence, though never worse than that of nations, is judged by the nations to be illegitimate.

IX. We had accepted uncritically the belief that technology is only good; that it cannot serve evil as well as good; that it cannot serve our enemies as well as ourselves; that it cannot be used to destroy what is good, including our homelands and our lives.

X. We had accepted too the corollary belief that an economy (either as a money economy or as a life-support system) that is global in extent, technologically complex, and centralized is invulnerable to terrorism, sabotage, or war, and that it is protectable by "national defense."

XI. We now have a clear, inescapable choice that we must make. We can continue to promote a global economic system of unlimited "free trade" among corporations, held together by long and highly vulnerable lines of communication and supply, but *now* recognizing that such a system will have to be protected by a hugely expensive police force that will be worldwide, whether maintained by one nation or several or all, and that such a police force will be effective precisely to the extent that it oversways the freedom and privacy of the citizens of every nation.

XII. Or we can promote a decentralized world economy which would have the aim of assuring to every nation and region a *local* self-sufficiency in life-supporting goods. This would not eliminate international trade, but it would tend toward a trade in surpluses after local needs had been met.

XIII. One of the gravest dangers to us now, second only to further terrorist attacks against our people, is that we will attempt to go on as before with the corporate program of global "free trade," whatever the cost in freedom and civil rights, without self-questioning or self-criticism or public debate.

XIV. This is why the substitution of rhetoric for thought, always a temptation in a national crisis, must be resisted by officials and citizens alike. It is hard for ordinary citizens to know what is actually happening in Washington in a time of such great trouble; for all we know, serious and difficult thought may be taking place there. But the talk that we are hearing from politicians, bureaucrats, and commentators has so far tended to reduce the complex problems now facing us to issues of unity, security, normality, and retaliation.

XV. National self-righteousness, like personal self-righteousness, is a mistake. It is misleading. It is a sign of weakness. Any war that we may make now against terrorism will come as a new installment in a history of war in which we have fully participated. We are not innocent of making war against civilian populations. The modern doctrine of such warfare was set forth and enacted by General William Tecumseh Sherman, who held that a civilian population could be declared guilty and rightly subjected to military punishment. We have never repudiated that doctrine.

XVI. It is a mistake also—as events since September 11 have shown—to suppose that a government can promote and participate in a global economy and at the same time act exclusively in its own interest by abrogating its international treaties and standing apart from international cooperation on moral issues.

XVII. And surely, in our country, under our Constitution, it is a fundamental error to suppose that any crisis or emergency can justify any form of political oppression. Since September 11, far too many public voices have presumed to "speak for us" in saying that Americans will gladly accept a reduction of freedom in exchange for greater "security." Some would, maybe. But some others would accept a reduction in security (and in global trade) far more willingly than they would accept any abridgement of our Constitutional rights.

XVIII. In a time such as this, when we have been seriously and most cruelly hurt by those who hate us, and when we must consider ourselves to be gravely threatened by those same people, it is hard to speak of the ways of peace and to remember that Christ enjoined us to love our enemies, but this is no less necessary for being difficult.

XIX. Even now we dare not forget that since the attack of Pearl Harbor—to which the present attack has been often and not usefully compared—we humans have suffered an almost uninterrupted sequence of wars, none of which has brought peace or made us more peaceable.

XX. The aim and result of war necessarily is not peace but victory, and any victory won by violence necessarily justifies the violence that won it and leads to further violence. If we are serious about innovation, must we not conclude that we need something new to replace our perpetual "war to end war"?

XXI. What leads to peace is not violence but peaceableness, which is not passivity, but an alert, informed, practiced, and active state of being. We should recognize that while we have extravagantly subsidized the means of war, we have almost totally neglected the ways of peaceableness. We have, for example, several national military academies, but not one peace academy. We have ignored the teachings and the examples of Christ, Gandhi, Martin Luther King, and other peaceable leaders. And here we have an inescapable duty to notice also that war is profitable, whereas the means of peaceableness, being cheap or free, make no money.

XXII. The key to peaceableness is continuous practice. It is wrong to suppose that we can exploit and impoverish the poorer countries, while arming them and instructing them in the newest means of war, and then reasonably expect them to be peaceable.

XXIII. We must not again allow public emotion or the public media to caricature our enemies. If our enemies are now to be some nations of Islam, then we should undertake to *know* those enemies. Our schools should begin to teach the histories, cultures, arts, and languages of the Islamic nations. And our leaders should have the humility and the wisdom to ask the reasons some of those people have for hating us.

XXIV. Starting with the economies of food and farming, we should promote at home, and encourage abroad, the ideal of local self-sufficiency. We should recognize that this is the surest, the safest, and the cheapest way for the world to live. We should not countenance the loss or destruction of any local capacity to produce necessary goods

XXV. We should reconsider and renew and extend our efforts to protect the natural foundations of the human economy: soil, water, and air. We should protect every intact ecosystem and watershed that we have left, and begin restoration of those that have been damaged.

XXVI. The complexity of our present trouble suggests as never before that we need to change our present concept of education. Education is not properly an industry, and its proper use is not to serve industries, either by job-training or by industry-subsidized research. Its proper use is to enable citizens to live lives that are economically, politically, socially, and culturally responsible. This cannot be done by gathering or "accessing" what we now call "information"—which is to say facts without context and therefore without priority. A proper education enables young people to put their lives in order, which means knowing what things are more important than other things; it means putting first things first.

XXVII. The first thing we must begin to teach our children (and learn ourselves) is that we cannot spend and consume endlessly. We have got to learn to save and conserve. We do need a "new economy," but one that is founded on thrift and care, on saving and conserving, not on excess and waste. An economy based on waste is inherently and hopelessly violent, and war is its inevitable by-product. We need a peaceable economy.

The Idea of a Local Economy

Let us begin by assuming what appears to be true: that the so-called "environmental crisis" is now pretty well established as a fact of our age. The problems of pollution, species extinction, loss of wilderness, loss of farmland, loss of topsoil may still be ignored or scoffed at, but they are not denied. Concern for these problems has acquired a certain standing, a measure of discussability, in the media and in some scientific, academic, and religious institutions.

This is good, of course; obviously, we can't hope to solve these problems without an increase of public awareness and concern. But in an age burdened with "publicity," we have to be aware also that as issues rise into popularity they rise also into the danger of oversimplification. To speak of this danger is especially necessary in confronting the destructiveness of our relationship to nature, which is the result, in the first place, of gross oversimplification.

The "environmental crisis" has happened because the human household or economy is in conflict at almost every point with the household of nature. We have built our household on the assumption that the natural household is simple and can be simply used. We have assumed increasingly over the last five hundred years that nature is merely a supply of "raw materials," and that we may safely possess those materials merely by taking them. This taking, as our technical means have increased, has involved always less reverence or respect, less gratitude, less local knowledge, and less skill. Our methodologies of land use have strayed from our old sympathetic attempts to imitate natural processes, and have come more and more to resemble the methodology of mining, even as mining itself has become more technologically powerful and more brutal.

And so we will be wrong if we attempt to correct what we perceive as "environmental" problems without correcting the economic oversimplification that caused them. This oversimplification is now either a matter of corporate behavior or of behavior under the influence of corporate behavior. This is sufficiently clear to many of us. What is not sufficiently clear, perhaps to any of us, is the extent of our complicity, as individuals and especially as individual consumers, in the behavior of the corporations.

What has happened is that most people in our country, and apparently most people in the "developed" world, have given proxies to the corporations to produce and provide *all* of their food, clothing, and shelter. Moreover, they are rapidly giving proxies to corporations or governments to provide entertainment, education, child care, care of the sick and the elderly, and many other kinds of "service" that once were carried on informally and inexpensively by individuals or households or communities. Our major economic practice, in short, is to delegate the practice to others.

The danger now is that those who are concerned will believe that the solution to the "environmental crisis" can be merely political—that the problems, being large, can be solved by large solutions generated by a few people to whom we will give our proxies to police the economic proxies that we have already given. The danger, in other words, is that people will think they have made a sufficient change if they have altered their "values," or had a "change of heart," or experienced a "spiritual awakening," and that such a change in passive consumers will cause appropriate changes in the public experts, politicians, and corporate executives to whom they have granted their political and economic proxies.

The trouble with this is that a proper concern for nature and our use of nature must be practiced not by our proxy-holders, but by ourselves. A change of heart or of values without a practice is only another pointless luxury of a passively consumptive way of life. The "environmental crisis," in fact, can be solved only if people, individually and in their communities, recover responsibility for their thoughtlessly given proxies. If people begin the effort to take back into their own power a significant portion of their economic responsibility, then their inevitable first discovery is that the "environmental crisis" is no such thing; it is not a crisis of our environs or surroundings; it is a crisis of our lives as individuals, as family members, as community members, and as citizens. We have an "environmental crisis" because we have consented to an economy in which by eating, drinking, working, resting, traveling, and enjoying ourselves we are destroying the natural, the god-given world.

We live, as we must sooner or later recognize, in an era of sentimental economics and, consequently, of sentimental politics. Sentimental communism holds in effect that everybody and everything should suffer for the good of "the many" who, though miserable in the present, will be happy in the future for exactly the same reasons that they are miserable in the present.

Sentimental capitalism is not so different from sentimental communism as the corporate and political powers claim. Sentimental capitalism holds in effect that everything small, local, private, personal, natural, good, and beautiful must be sacrificed in the interest of the "free market" and the great corporations, which will bring unprecedented security and happiness to "the many"—in, of course, the future.

These forms of political economy may be described as sentimental because they depend absolutely upon a political faith for which there is no justification, and because they issue a cold check on the virtue of political and/or economic rulers. They seek, that is, to preserve the gullibility of the people by appealing to a fund of political virtue that does not exist. Communism and "free market" capitalism both are modern versions of oligarchy. In their propaganda, both justify violent means by good ends, which always are put beyond reach by the violence of the means. The trick is to define the end vaguely—"the greatest good of the greatest number" or "the benefit of the many"—and keep it at a distance.

The fraudulence of these oligarchic forms of economy is in their principle of displacing whatever good they recognize (as well as their debts) from the present to the future. Their success depends upon persuading people, first, that whatever they have now is no good, and second, that the promised good is certain to be achieved in the future. This obviously contradicts the principle—common, I believe, to all the religious traditions—that if ever we are going to do good to one another, then the time to do it is now; we are to receive no reward for promising to do it in the future. And both communism and capitalism have found such principles to be a great embarrassment. If you are presently occupied in destroying every good thing in sight in order to do good in the future, it is inconvenient to have people saying things like "Love thy neighbor as thyself" or "Sentient beings are numberless, I vow to save them." Communists and capitalists alike, "liberal" and "conservative" capitalists alike, have needed to replace religion with some form of determinism, so that they can say to their victims, "I am doing this because I can't do otherwise. It is not my fault. It is inevitable." The wonder is how often organized religion has gone along with this lie.

The idea of an economy based upon several kinds of ruin may seem a contradiction in terms, but in fact such an economy is possible, as we see. It is possible however, on one implacable condition: the only future good that it assuredly leads to is that it will destroy itself. And how does it disguise this outcome from its subjects, its short-term beneficiaries, and its victims? It does so by false accounting. It substitutes for the real economy, by which we build and maintain (or do not maintain) our house-hold, a symbolic economy of money, which in the long run, because of the self-interested manipulations of the "controlling interests," cannot symbolize or account for anything but itself. And so we have before us the specta-cle of unprecedented "prosperity" and "economic growth" in a land of degraded farms, forests, ecosystems, and watersheds, polluted air, failing families, and perish-ing communities.

This moral and economic absurdity exists for the sake of the allegedly "free" market, the single principle of which is this: commodities will be produced wherever they can be produced at the lowest cost, and consumed wherever they will bring the highest price. To make too cheap and sell too high has always been the program of industrial capitalism. The idea of the global "free market" is merely capitalism's so-far-successful attempt to enlarge the geographic scope of its greed, and moreover to give to its greed the status of a "right" within its presumptive territory. The global "free market" is free to the corporations precisely because it dissolves the boundaries of the old national colonialisms, and replaces them with a new colonialism without restraints or boundaries. It is pretty much as if all the rabbits have now been forbidden to have holes, thereby "freeing" the hounds.

The "right" of a corporation to exercise its economic power without restraint is construed, by the partisans of the "free market," as a form of freedom, a political liberty implied presumably by the right of individual citizens to own and use property.

But the "free market" idea introduces into government a sanction of an inequality that is not implicit in any idea of democratic liberty: namely that the "free market" is freest to those who have the most money, and is not free at all to those with little or no money. Wal-Mart, for example, as a large corporation "freely" competing against local, privately owned businesses has virtually all the freedom, and its small competitors virtually none.

To make too cheap and sell too high, there are two requirements. One is that you must have a lot of consumers with surplus money and unlimited wants. For the time being, there are plenty of these consumers in the "developed" countries. The problem, for the time being easily solved, is simply to keep them relatively affluent and dependent on purchased supplies.

The other requirement is that the market for labor and raw materials should remain depressed relative to the market for retail commodities. This means that the supply of workers should exceed demand, and that the land-using economy should be allowed or encouraged to overproduce.

To keep the cost of labor low, it is necessary first to entice or force country people everywhere in the world to move into the cities—in the manner prescribed by the United States' Committee for Economic Development after World War II—and second, to continue to introduce labor-replacing technology. In this way it is possible to maintain a "pool" of people who are in the threatening position of being mere consumers, landless and also poor, and who therefore are eager to go to work for low wages—precisely the condition of migrant farm workers in the United States.

To cause the land-using economies to overproduce is even simpler. The farmers and other workers in the world's land-using economies, by and large, are not organized. They are therefore unable to control production in order to secure just prices. Individual producers must go individually to the market and take for their produce simply whatever they are paid. They have no power to bargain or make demands. Increasingly, they must sell, not to neighbors or to neighboring towns and cities, but to large and remote corporations. There is no competition among the buyers (supposing there is more than one), who are organized, and are "free" to exploit the advantage of low prices. Low prices encourage over-production as producers attempt to make up their losses "on volume," and overproduction inevitably makes for low prices. The land-using economies thus spiral down-ward as the money economy of the exploiters spirals upward. If economic attrition in the land-using popula-tion becomes so severe as to threaten production, then governments can subsidize production without produc-tion controls, which necessarily will encourage overpro-duction, which will lower prices—and so the subsidy to rural   producers becomes, in effect, a subsidy to the purchasing corporations. In the land-using economies production is further cheapened by destroying, with low prices and low standards of quality, the cultural impera-tives for good work and land stewardship.

This sort of exploitation, long familiar in the foreign and domestic economies and the colonialism of modern nations, has now become "the global economy," which is the property of a few supranational corporations. The economic theory used to justify the global economy in its "free market" version is again perfectly groundless and sentimental. The idea is that what is good for the corpo-rations will sooner or later—though not of course immediately—be good for everybody.

That sentimentality is based in turn, upon a fantasy: the proposition that the great corporations, in "freely" competing with one another for raw materials, labor, and marketshare, will drive each other indefinitely, not only toward greater "efficiencies" of manufacture, but also toward higher bids for raw materials and labor and lower prices to consumers. As a result, all the world's people will be economically secure—in the future. It would be hard to object to such a proposition if only it were true.

But one knows, in the first place, that "efficiency" in manufacture always means reducing labor costs by replacing workers with cheaper workers or with machines.

In the second place, the "law of competition" does *not* imply that many competitors will compete indefinitely. The law of competition is a simple paradox: Competition destroys competition. The law of competition implies that many competitors, competing without restraint, will ultimately and inevitably reduce the number of competitors to one. The law of competition, in short, is the law of war.

In the third place, the global economy is based upon cheap long-distance transportation, without which it is not possible to move goods from the point of cheapest origin to the point of highest sale. And cheap long-distance transportation is the basis of the idea that regions and nations should abandon any measure of economic self-sufficiency in order to specialize in production for export of the few commodities or the single commodity that can be most cheaply produced. Whatever may be said for the "efficiency" of such a system, its result (and I assume, its purpose) is to destroy local production capacities, local diversity, and local economic independence.

This idea of a global "free market" economy, despite its obvious moral flaws and its dangerous practical weaknesses, is now the ruling orthodoxy of the age. Its propaganda is subscribed to and distributed by most political leaders, editorial writers, and other "opinion makers." The powers that be, while continuing to budget huge sums for "national defense," have apparently abandoned any idea of national or local self-sufficiency, even in food. They also have given up the idea that a national or local government might justly place restraints upon economic activity in order to protect its land and its people.

The global economy is now institutionalized in the World Trade Organization, which was set up, without election anywhere, to rule international trade on behalf of the "free market"—which is to say on behalf of the supranational corporations—and to *over*rule, in secret sessions, any national or regional law that conflicts with the "free market." The corporate program of global free trade and the presence of the World Trade Organization have legitimized extreme forms of expert thought. We are told confidently that if Kentucky loses its milk-producing capacity to Wisconsin, that will be a "success story." Experts such as Stephen C. Blank, of the University of California, Davis, have proposed that "developed" countries, such as the United States and the

United Kingdom, where food can no longer be produced cheaply enough, should give up agriculture altogether.

The folly at the root of this foolish economy began with the idea that a corporation should be regarded, legally, as "a person." But the limitless destructiveness of this economy comes about precisely because a corporation is *not* a person. A corporation, essentially, is a pile of money to which a number of persons have sold their moral allegiance. As such, unlike a person, a corporation does not age. It does not arrive, as most persons finally do, at a realization of the shortness and smallness of human lives; it does not come to see the future as the lifetime of the children and grandchildren of anybody in particular. It can experience no personal hope or remorse, no change of heart. It cannot humble itself. It goes about its business as if it were immortal, with the single purpose of becoming a bigger pile of money. The stockholders essentially are usurers, people who "let their money work for them," expecting high pay in return for causing others to work for low pay. The World Trade Organization enlarges the old idea of the corporation-as-person by giving the global corporate economy the status of a super government with the power to overrule nations.

I don't mean to say, of course, that all corporate executives and stockholders are bad people. I am only saying that all of them are very seriously implicated in a bad economy.

Unsurprisingly, among people who wish to preserve things other than money—for instance, every region's native capacity to produce essential goods—there is a growing perception that the global "free market" economy is inherently an enemy to the natural world, to human health and freedom, to industrial workers, and to farmers and others in the land-use economies; and furthermore, that it is inherently an enemy to good work and good economic practice.

I believe that this perception is correct and that it can be shown to be correct merely by listing the assumptions implicit in the idea that corporations should be "free" to buy low and sell high in the world at large. These assumptions, so far as I can make them out, are as follows:

1. That stable and preserving relationships among people, places, and things do not matter and are of no worth.

2. That cultures and religions have no legitimate practical or economic concerns.

3. That there is no conflict between the "free market" and political freedom, and no connection between political democracy and economic democracy.

4. That there can be no conflict between economic advantage and economic justice.

5. That there is no conflict between greed and ecological or bodily health.

6. That there is no conflict between self-interest and public service.

7. That the loss or destruction of the capacity anywhere to produce necessary goods does not matter and involves no cost.

8. That it is all right for a nation's or a region's subsistence to be foreign based, dependent on long-distance transport, and entirely controlled by corporations.

9. That, therefore, wars over commodities—our recent Gulf War, for example—are legitimate and permanent economic functions.

10. That this sort of sanctioned violence is justified also by the predominance of centralized systems of production, supply, communications, and transportation, which are extremely vulnerable not only to acts of war between nations, but also to sabotage and terrorism.

11. That it is all right for poor people in poor countries to work at poor wages to produce goods for export to affluent people in rich countries.

12. That there is no danger and no cost in the proliferation of exotic pests, weeds, and diseases that accompany international trade and that increase with the volume of trade.

13. That an economy is a machine, of which people are merely the interchangeable parts. One has no choice but to do the work (if any) that the economy prescribes, and to accept the prescribed wage.

14. That, therefore, vocation is a dead issue. One does not do the work that one chooses to do because one is called to it by Heaven or by one's natural or god-given abilities, but does instead the work that is determined and imposed by the economy. Any work is all right as long as one gets paid for it.

These assumptions clearly prefigure a condition of total economy. A total economy is one in which everything—"life forms," for instance, or the "right to pollute"—is "private property" and has a price and is for sale. In a total economy significant and sometimes critical choices that once belonged to individuals or communities become the property of corporations. A total economy, operating internationally, necessarily shrinks the powers of state and national governments, not only because those governments have signed over significant powers to an international bureaucracy or because political leaders become the paid hacks of the corporations but also because political processes—and especially democratic processes—are too slow to react to unrestrained economic and technological development on a global scale. And when state and national governments begin to act in effect as agents of the global economy, selling their people for low wages and their people's products for low prices, then the rights and liberties of citizenship must necessarily shrink. A total economy is an unrestrained taking of profits from the disintegration of nations, communities, households, landscapes, and ecosystems. It licenses symbolic or artificial wealth to "grow" by means of the destruction of the real wealth of all the world.

Among the many costs of the total economy, the loss of the principle of vocation is probably the most symptomatic and, from a cultural standpoint, the most critical. It is by the replacement of vocation with economic determinism that the exterior workings of a total economy destroy the character and culture also from the inside.

In an essay on the origin of civilization in traditional cultures, Ananda K. Coomaraswamy wrote that "the principle of justice is the same throughout…[it is] that each member of the community should perform the task for which he is fitted by nature…." The two ideas, justice and vocation, are inseparable. That is why Coomaraswamy spoke of industrialism as "the mammon of injustice," incompatible with civilization. It is by way of the principle and practice of vocation that sanctity and reverence enter into the human economy. It was thus possible for traditional cultures to conceive that "to work is to pray."

Aware of industrialism's potential for destruction, as well as the considerable political danger of great concentrations of wealth and power in industrial corporations, American leaders developed, and for a while used, the means of limiting and restraining such concentrations, and of somewhat equitably distributing wealth and property. The means were: laws against trusts and monopolies, the principle of collective bargaining, the concept of one-hundred-percent parity between the land-using and the manufacturing economies, and the progressive income tax. And to protect domestic producers and production capacities it is possible for governments to impose tariffs on cheap imported goods. These means are justified by the government's obligation to protect the lives, livelihoods, and freedoms of its citizens. There is, then, no necessity or inevitability requiring our government to sacrifice the livelihoods of our small farmers, small business people, and workers, along with our domestic economic independence to the global "free market." But now all of these means are either weakened or in disuse. The global economy is intended as a means of subverting them.

In default of government protections against the total economy of the supranational corporations, people are where they have been many times before: in danger of losing their economic security and their freedom, both at once. But at the same time the means of defending themselves belongs to them in the form of a venerable principle: powers not exercised by government return to the people. If the government does not propose to protect the lives, livelihoods, and freedoms of its people, then the people must think about protecting themselves.

How are they to protect themselves? There seems, really, to be only one way, and that is to develop and put into practice the idea of a local economy—something that growing numbers of people are now doing. For several good reasons, they are beginning with the idea of a local food economy. People are trying to find ways to shorten the distance between producers and consumers, to make the connections between the two more direct, and to make this local economic activity a benefit to the local community. They are trying to learn to use the consumer economies of local towns and cities to preserve the livelihoods of local farm families and farm communities. They want to use the local economy to give consumers an influence over the kind and quality of their food, and to preserve and enhance the local landscapes. They want to give everybody in the local community a direct, long-term interest in the prosperity, health, and beauty of their homeland. This is the only way presently available to make the total economy less total. It was once, I believe, the only way to make a national or a colonial economy less total. But now the necessity is greater.

I am assuming that there is a valid line of thought leading from the idea of the total economy to the idea of a local economy. I assume that the first thought may be a recognition of one's ignorance and vulnerability as a consumer in the total economy. As such a consumer, one does not know the history of the products that one uses. Where, exactly, did they come from? Who produced them? What toxins were used in their production? What were the human and ecological costs of producing them and then of disposing of them? One sees that such questions cannot be answered easily, and perhaps not at all. Though one is shopping amid an astonishing variety of products, one is denied certain significant choices. In such a state of economic ignorance it is not possible to choose products that were produced locally or with reasonable kindness toward people and toward nature. Nor is it possible for such consumers to influence production for the better. Consumers who feel a prompting toward land stewardship find that in this economy they can have no stewardly practice. To be a consumer in the total economy, one must agree to be totally ignorant, totally passive, and totally dependent on distant supplies and self-interested suppliers.

And then, perhaps, one begins to *see* from a local point of view. One begins to ask, What is here, what is in me, that can lead to something better? From a local point of view, one can see that a global "free market" economy is possible only if nations and localities accept or ignore the inherent instability of a production economy based on exports and a consumer economy based on imports. An export economy is beyond local influence, and so is an import economy. And cheap long-distance transport is possible only if granted cheap fuel, international peace, control of terrorism, prevention of sabotage, and the solvency of the international economy.

Perhaps one also begins to see the difference between a small local business that must share the fate of the local community and a large absentee corporation that is set up to escape the fate of the local community by ruining the local community.

So far as I can see, the idea of a local economy rests upon only two principles: neighborhood and subsistence.

In a viable neighborhood, neighbors ask themselves what they can do or provide for one another, and they find answers that they and their place can afford. This, and nothing else, is the *practice* of neighborhood. This practice must be, in part, charitable, but it must also be economic, and the economic part must be equitable; there is a significant charity in just prices.

Of course, everything needed locally cannot be

produced locally. But a viable neighborhood is a community; and a viable community is made up of neighbors who cherish and protect what they have in common. This is the principle of subsistence. A viable community, like a viable farm, protects its own production capacities. It does not import products that it can produce for itself. And it does not export local products until local needs have been met. The economic products of a viable community are understood either as belonging to the community's subsistence or as surplus, and only the surplus is considered to be marketable abroad. A community, if it is to be viable, cannot think of producing solely for export, and it cannot permit importers to use cheaper labor and goods from other places to destroy the local capacity to produce goods that are needed locally. In charity, moreover, it must refuse to import goods that are produced at the cost of human or ecological degradation elsewhere. This principle applies not just to localities, but to regions and nations as well.

The principles of neighborhood and subsistence will be disparaged by the globalists as "protectionism"—and that is exactly what it is. It is a protectionism that is just and sound, because it protects local producers and is the best assurance of adequate supplies to local consumers. And the idea that local needs should be met first and only surpluses exported does not imply any prejudice against charity toward people in other places or trade with them. The principle of neighborhood at home always implies the principle of charity abroad. And the principle of subsistence is in fact the best guarantee of giveable or marketable surpluses. This kind of protection is not "isolationism."

Albert Schweitzer, who knew well the economic situation in the colonies of Africa, wrote nearly sixty years ago: "Whenever the timber trade is good, permanent famine reigns in the Ogowe region because the villagers abandon their farms to fell as many trees as possible." We should notice especially that the goal of production was "as many...as possible." And Schweitzer makes my point exactly: "These people could achieve true wealth if they could develop their agriculture and trade to meet their own needs." Instead they produced timber for export to "the world economy," which made them dependent upon imported goods that they bought with money earned from their exports. They gave up their local means of subsistence, and imposed the false standard of a foreign demand ("as many trees as possible") upon their forests. They thus became helplessly dependent on an economy over which they had no control.

Such was the fate of the native people under the African colonialism of Schweitzer's time. Such is, and can only be, the fate of everybody under the global colonialism of our time. Schweitzer's description of the colonial economy of the Ogowe region is in principle not different from the rural economy now in Kentucky or Iowa or Wyoming. A total economy for all practical purposes is a total government. The "free trade," from the standpoint of the corporate economy brings "unprecedented economic growth," from the standpoint of the land and its local populations, and ultimately from the standpoint of the cities, is destruction and slavery. Without prosperous local economies, the people have no power and the land no voice.

In Distrust of Movements

I have had with my friend Wes Jackson a number of
useful conversations about the necessity of getting out of
movements—even movements that have seemed necessary and dear to us—when they have lapsed into self-
righteousness and self-betrayal, as movements seem
almost invariably to do. People in movements too readily
learn to deny to others the rights and privileges they
demand for themselves. They too easily become unable
to mean their own language, as when a "peace movement" becomes violent. They often become too specialized, as if finally they cannot help taking refuge in the
pinhole vision of the institutional intellectuals. They
almost always fail to be radical enough, dealing finally in
effects rather than causes. Or they deal with single issues
or single solutions, as if to assure themselves that they

will not be radical enough.

And so I must declare my dissatisfaction with movements to promote soil conservation or clean water or clean air or wilderness preservation or sustainable agriculture or community health or the welfare of children. Worthy as these and other goals may be, they cannot be achieved alone. I am dissatisfied with such efforts because they are too specialized, they are not comprehensive enough, they are not radical enough, they virtually predict their own failure by implying that we can remedy or control effects while leaving causes in place. Ultimately, I think, they are insincere; they propose that the trouble is caused by *other* people; they would like to change policy but not behavior.

The worst danger may be that a movement will lose its language either to its own confusion about meaning and practice, or to preemption by its enemies. I remember, for example, my naïve confusion at learning that it was possible for advocates of organic agriculture to look upon the "organic method" as an end in itself. To me, organic farming was attractive both as a way of conserving nature and as a strategy of survival for small farmers. Imagine my surprise in discovering that there could be huge "organic" monocultures. And so I was not too surprised by the recent attempt of the United States Department of Agriculture to appropriate the "organic" label for food irradiation, genetic engineering, and other desecrations of the corporate food economy. Once we allow our language to mean anything that anybody wants it to mean, it becomes impossible to mean what we say. When "homemade" ceases to mean neither more nor less than "made at home," then it means anything, which is to say that it means nothing.

As you see, I have good reasons for declining to name the movement I think I am a part of. I am reconciled to the likelihood that from time to time it will name itself and have slogans, but I am not going to use its slogans or call it by any of its names.

Let us suppose that we have a Nameless Movement for Better Land Use and that we know we must try to keep it active, responsive, and intelligent for a long time. What must we do?

What we must do above all, I think, is try to see the problem in its full size and difficulty. If we are concerned about land abuse, then we must see that this is an economic problem. Every economy is, by definition, a land-using economy. If we are using our land wrong, then something is wrong with our economy. This is difficult. It becomes more difficult when we recognize that, in modern times, every one of us is a member of the economy of everybody else.

But if we are concerned about land abuse, we have begun a profound work of economic criticism. Study of the history of land use (and any local history will do) informs us that we have had for a long time an economy that thrives by undermining its own foundations. Industrialism, which is the name of our economy, and which is now virtually the only economy of the world, has been from its beginnings in a state of riot. It is based squarely upon the principle of violence toward everything on which it depends, and it has not mattered whether the form of industrialism was communist or capitalist or whatever; the violence toward nature, human communities, traditional agricultures, local economies has been constant. The bad news is coming in, literally, from all over the world. Can such an economy be fixed without being radically changed? I don't think it can.

The Captains of Industry have always counseled the rest of us "to be realistic." Let us, therefore, be realistic. Is it realistic to assume that the present economy would be just fine if only it would stop poisoning the air and water, or if only it would stop soil erosion, or if only it would stop degrading watersheds and forest ecosystems, or if only it would stop seducing children, or if only it would quit buying politicians, or if only it would give women and favored minorities an equitable share of the loot? Realism, I think is a very limited program, but it informs us at least that we should not look for bird eggs in a cuckoo clock.

Or we can show the hopelessness of single-issue causes and single-issue movements by following a line of thought such as this: We need a continuous supply of uncontaminated water. Therefore, we need (among other things) soil-and-water-conserving ways of agriculture and forestry that are not dependent on monoculture, toxic chemicals, or the indifference and violence that always accompany big-scale industrial enterprises on the land. Therefore, we need diversified, small-scale land economies that are dependent on people. Therefore, we need people with the knowledge, skills, motives, and attitudes required by diversified, small-scale land economies. And all this is clear and comfortable enough, until we recognize the question we have come to: *Where are the people?*

Well, all of us who live in the suffering rural land-scapes of the United States know that most people are available to those landscapes only recreationally. We see them bicycling or boating or hiking or camping or hunting or fishing or driving along and looking around. They do not, in Mary Austin's phrase, "summer and winter with the land." They are unacquainted with the land's human and natural economies. Though people have not progressed beyond the need to eat food and drink water and wear clothes and live in houses, most people have progressed beyond the domestic arts—the husbandry and wifery of the world—by which those needful things are produced and conserved. In fact, the comparative few who still practice that necessary husbandry and wifery often are inclined to apologize for doing so, having been carefully taught in our education system that those arts are degrading and unworthy of people's talents. Educated minds, in the modern era, are unlikely to know anything about food and drink, clothing and shelter. In merely taking these things for granted, the modern educated mind reveals itself also to be as superstitious a mind as ever has existed in the world. What could be more superstitious than the idea that money brings forth food?

I am not suggesting, of course, that everybody ought to be a farmer or a forester. Heaven forbid! I am suggesting that most people now are living on the far side of a broken connection, and that this is potentially catastrophic. Most people are now fed, clothed, and sheltered from sources toward which they feel no gratitude and exercise no responsibility. There is no significant urban constituency, no formidable consumer lobby, no noticeable political leadership for good land use practices, for good farming and good forestry, for restoration of abused land, or for halting the destruction of land by so-called "development."

We are involved now in a profound failure of imagination. Most of us cannot imagine the wheat beyond the bread, or the farmer beyond the wheat, or the farm beyond the farmer, or the history beyond the farm. Most people cannot imagine the forest and the forest economy that produced their houses and furniture and paper; or the landscapes, the streams, and the weather that fill their pitchers and bathtubs and swimming pools with water. Most people appear to assume that when they have paid their money for these things they have entirely met their obligations.

Money does not bring forth food. Neither does the technology of the food system. Food comes from nature and from the work of people. If the supply of food is to be continuous for a long time, then people must work in harmony with nature. That means that people must find the right answers to a lot of hard practical questions. The same applies to forestry and the possibility of a continuous supply of timber.

One way we could describe the task ahead of us is by saying that we need to enlarge the consciousness and the conscience of the economy. Our economy needs to know—and care—what it is doing. This is revolutionary, of course, if you have a taste for revolution, but it is also a matter of common sense.

Undoubtedly some people will want to start a movement to bring this about. They probably will call it the Movement to Teach the Economy What It Is Doing— the MTEWIID. Despite my very considerable uneasiness, I will agree to this, but on three conditions.

My first condition is that this movement should begin by giving up all hope and belief in piecemeal, one-shot solutions. The present scientific quest for odorless hog manure should give us sufficient proof that the specialist is no longer with us. Even now, after centuries of reductionist propaganda, the world is still intricate and vast, as dark as it is light, a place of mystery, where we cannot do one thing without doing many things, or put two things together without putting many things together. Water quality, for example, cannot be improved without improving farming and forestry, but farming and forestry cannot be improved without improving the education of consumers—and so on.

The proper business of a human economy is to make one whole thing of ourselves and this world. To make ourselves into a practical wholeness with the land under our feet is maybe not altogether possible—how would *we* know?—but, as a goal, it at least carries us beyond *hubris*, beyond the utterly groundless assumption that we can subdivide our present great failure into a thousand separate problems that can be fixed by a thousand task forces of academic and bureaucratic specialists. That program has been given more than a fair chance to prove itself, and we ought to know by now that it won't work.

My second condition is that the people in this movement (the MTEWIID) should take full responsibility for themselves as members of the economy. If we are going to teach the economy what it is doing, then we need to learn what we are doing. This is going to have to be a private movement as well as a public one. If it is unrealistic to expect wasteful industries to be conservers, then obviously we must lead in part the public life of complainers, petitioners, protesters, advocates, and supporters of stricter regulations and saner policies. But that is not enough. If it is unreasonable to expect a bad economy to try to become a good one, then *we* must go to work to build a good economy. It is appropriate that this duty should fall to us, for good economic behavior is more possible for us than it is for the great corporations with their miseducated managers and their greedy and oblivious stockholders. Because it is possible for us, we must try in every way we can to make good economic sense in our own lives, in our households, and in our communities. We must do more for ourselves and our neighbors. We must learn to spend our money with our friends and not with our enemies. But to do this, it is necessary to renew local economies, and revive the domestic arts. In seeking to change our economic use of the world, we are seeking inescapably to change our lives. The outward harmony that we desire between our economy and the world depends finally upon an inward harmony between our own hearts and the originating spirit that is the life of all creatures, a spirit as near us as our flesh and yet forever beyond the measures of this obsessively measuring age. We can grow good wheat and make good bread only if we understand that we do not live by bread alone.

My third condition is that this movement should content itself to be poor. We need to find cheap solutions, solutions within the reach of everybody, and the availability of a lot of money prevents the discovery of cheap solutions. The solutions of modern medicine and modern agriculture are all staggeringly expensive, and this is caused in part, and maybe altogether, because of the availability of huge sums of money for medical and agricultural research.

Too much money, moreover, attracts administrators and experts as sugar attracts ants—look at what is happening in our universities. We should not envy rich movements that are organized and led by an alternative bureaucracy living on the problems it is supposed to solve. We want a movement that is a movement because it is advanced by all its members in their daily lives.

Now, having completed this very formidable list of the problems and difficulties, fears and fearful hopes that lie ahead of us, I am relieved to see that I have been preparing myself all along to end by saying something cheerful. What I have been talking about is the possibility of renewing human respect for this earth and all the good, useful, and beautiful things that come from it. I have made it clear, I hope, that I don't think this respect can be adequately enacted or conveyed by tipping our hats to nature or by representing natural loveliness in art or by prayers of thanksgiving or by preserving tracts of wilderness—although I recommend all those things. The respect I mean can be given only by using well the world's goods that are given to us. This good use, which renews respect—which is the only currency, so to speak, of respect—also renews our pleasure. The callings and disciplines that I have spoken of as the domestic arts are stationed all along the way from the farm to the prepared dinner, from the forest to the dinner table, from stewardship of the land to hospitality to friends and strangers. These arts are as demanding and gratifying, as instructive and as pleasing, as the so-called "fine arts." To learn them is, I believe, the work that is our profoundest calling. Our reward is that they will enrich our lives and make us glad.

Wendell Berry

An essayist, novelist, poet, and farmer, Wendell Berry is the author of more than thirty books including, most recently *Life Is a Miracle* and *Jayber Crow.* He is a long-time member of The Orion Society's advisory board and the past recipient of the T. S. Eliot Award, The Orion Society's John Hay Award, the Lyndhurst Prize, and the Aiken-Taylor Award for Poetry from The Sewanee review. He lives and works with his wife Tanya, on their farm in Port Royal, Kentucky.

The Orion Society

The Orion Society's mission is to inform, inspire, and engage individuals and grassroots organizations across North America in becoming a significant cultural force for healing nature and community. Our programs and publications include:

Orion **magazine:** "America's finest environmental magazine" (Boston Globe), is an influential forum for re-imagining humanity's relationship to nature, featuring America's foremost writers and artists.

Orion Afield **magazine:** An award-winning magazine that shares news and success stories from the rapidly expanding grassroots environmental movement.

OrionOnline.org: Orion's website features powerful and poignant multimedia content, including web-exclusive articles, videos, and art exhibitions, which are publicized via our popular e-mail updates.

Orion Institutes: These workshops and seminars provide training in Orion-pioneered place-based studies for educators, grassroots professionals, and others.

Orion books: Orion's books range from the popular Nature Literacy Series of educational resources to collections of essays by America's finest writers.

Orion Grassroots Network: With 500 member organizations, the Orion Grassroots Network is a fast-growing association of environmental and community organizations across North America.

The Orion Society is a not for profit organization.

Learn more about Orion, or purchase additional copies of *In the Presence of Fear*, at
www.oriononline.org

For information on bulk orders of ten or more copies of *In the Presence of Fear*, please call 888/909-6568.